Sierra Nevada Network White Pine Community Dynamics 2011 Annual Monitoring Report

Sequoia and Kings Canyon National Parks (SEKI) and Yosemite National Park (YOSE)

Natural Resource Data Series NPS/SIEN/NRDS—2012/405

Devin S. Stucki

National Park Service
Upper Columbia Basin Network Inventory and Monitoring Program
Craters of the Moon National Monument and Preserve
Arco, ID 83213

Shawn T. McKinney

USGS Maine Cooperative Fish & Wildlife Research Unit
Department of Wildlife Ecology
University of Maine
5755 Nutting Hall
Orono, ME 04469-5755

Jonathan C.B. Nesmith

National Park Service
Sierra Nevada Network Inventory and Monitoring Program
Sequoia National Park
47050 Generals Highway
Three Rivers, CA 93271

November 2012

U.S. Department of the Interior
National Park Service
Natural Resource Stewardship and Science
Fort Collins, Colorado

The National Park Service, Natural Resource Stewardship and Science office in Fort Collins, Colorado publishes a range of reports that address natural resource topics of interest and applicability to a broad audience in the National Park Service and others in natural resource management, including scientists, conservation and environmental constituencies, and the public.

The Natural Resource Data Series is intended for the timely release of basic data sets and data summaries. Care has been taken to assure accuracy of raw data values, but a thorough analysis and interpretation of the data has not been completed. Consequently, the initial analyses of data in this report are provisional and subject to change.

All manuscripts in the series receive the appropriate level of peer review to ensure that the information is scientifically credible, technically accurate, appropriately written for the intended audience, and designed and published in a professional manner.

This report received informal peer review by subject-matter experts who were not directly involved in the collection, analysis, or reporting of the data. Data in this report were collected and summarized using methods based on established, peer-reviewed protocols.

Views, statements, findings, conclusions, recommendations, and data in this report do not necessarily reflect views and policies of the National Park Service, U.S. Department of the Interior. Mention of trade names or commercial products does not constitute endorsement or recommendation for use by the U.S. Government.

This report is available from the Sierra Nevada Network Inventory and Monitoring Program at (http://science.nature.nps.gov/im/units/sien/) and the Natural Resource Publications Management website (http://www.nature.nps.gov/publications/nrpm/) on the internet.

Please cite this publication as:

Stucki, D. S., S. T. McKinney, and J. C. B. Nesmith. 2012. Sierra Nevada Network white pine community dynamics 2011 annual monitoring report: Sequoia and Kings Canyon National Parks (SEKI) and Yosemite National Park (YOSE). Natural Resource Data Series NPS/SIEN/NRDS—2012/405. National Park Service, Fort Collins, Colorado.

NPS 963/117644, November 2012

Contents

	Page
Figures	iv
Tables	iv
Executive Summary	v
Acknowledgments	vii
Background and Objectives	1
Whitebark Pine	1
Foxtail Pine	2
Objectives	3
Methods	5
Sampling Frame	5
Frequency and Timing of Sampling	9
Plot Layout	9
Plot Measurements	10
2011 Sampling Logistics	12
Results and Discussion	13
YOSE	13
SEKI	13
Summary	14
Suggested/Required Changes to the Protocol	15
Literature Cited	16
Appendix 1	20

Figures

Page

Figure 1. Distribution of whitebark pine, limber pine, and foxtail pine and locations of three Pacific West Region networks and associated parks. 3

Figure 2. Whitebark pine sampling frame and GRTS sample of plot locations for Sequoia and Kings Canyon National Parks. 6

Figure 3. Foxtail pine sampling frame and GRTS sample of plot locations for Sequoia and Kings Canyon National Parks. 7

Figure 4. Whitebark pine sampling frame and GRTS sample of plot locations for Yosemite National Park. 8

Figure 5. 50 x 50 m permanent plot layout used in SIEN white pine monitoring. 10

Tables

Page

Table 1. Revisit design for monitoring white pine species in the Sierra Nevada Network. 9

Table 2. Relationship among variables, data, and objectives, from McKinney et al. (2012a). 11

Table 3. Summary statistics on whitebark pine plots installed at YOSE in 2011 13

Table 4. Summary statistics on foxtail pine plots installed at SEKI in 2011 14

Executive Summary

The Sierra Nevada Network (SIEN) has identified 14 priority park vital signs, indicators of ecosystem health, which represent a broad suite of ecological phenomena operating across multiple temporal and spatial scales. The intent has been to monitor a balanced and integrated group of vital signs that meets the needs of current park management and that will also be able to accommodate unanticipated environmental conditions and management issues in the future. White pine tree species in Sequoia and Kings Canyon National Parks (SEKI) and Yosemite National Park (YOSE) are vulnerable to invasive pathogens as well as other stressors, including native pests and climate change-induced drought, and have been recognized as a high priority vital sign for SIEN. Currently, populations of whitebark pine (*Pinus albicaulis*) and foxtail pine (*P. balfouriana*), as well as their respective plant communities, are in better ecological condition in the Sierra Nevada compared to populations in the Cascades and Rocky Mountains (Millar et al. 2012). However, the observed steeply declining trends in white pine populations in the northern Cascades and Rocky Mountains, coupled with the identification of key stressors in SIEN parks, is a significant cause for concern about the future status of these ecologically valuable communities. Monitoring white pine forest community dynamics will allow for early detection of downward trends and indicate the need for subsequent management intervention. Moreover, information from this monitoring project will contribute meaningfully to the broader regional assessment of the status and trends of white pine species across western North America. White pine monitoring in SIEN is being closely coordinated with limber pine (*P. flexilis*) in the Upper Columbia Basin Network (UCBN), and whitebark pine in the Klamath Network (KLMN), including the use of a common protocol.

This report documents the results of the first year of protocol implementation in SEKI and YOSE in 2011. Our goal was to establish the first of three rotating panels (panel 1) for each species-park population: YOSE-whitebark pine, SEKI-whitebark pine, and SEKI-foxtail pine. Each panel consists of 16 permanent 50 x 50 m (2,500 m^2) plots that were randomly selected for each of the three populations. Thus, there will be a total of 48 whitebark pine plots in YOSE, 48 whitebark pine plots in SEKI, and 48 foxtail pine plots in SEKI. Data from plot surveys will be used to determine white pine forest community dynamics in SEKI and YOSE, including changes in tree species composition, forest structure, rates of birth, death and growth. Factors affecting tree health and reproduction including incidence and severity of white pine blister rust (*Cronartium ribicola*) infection, mountain pine beetle (*Dendroctonus ponderosae*) infestation, dwarf mistletoe (*Arceuthobium spp.*) infection, canopy kill, and female cone production are also recorded.

From late July to late August 2011, we established 11 whitebark pine plots in YOSE, and from late August to early September, we established 7 foxtail pine plots in SEKI. We did not establish any whitebark pine plots in SEKI due to a crew-related accident which occurred on September 8th and resulted in the suspension of field work for the remainder of the season.

In the 11 YOSE whitebark pine plots, 1,039 whitebark pines trees and 706 other conifers were sampled. An additional 20 dead trees of unidentified species were also sampled. Indications of white pine blister rust or dwarf mistletoe were not found, but there was one live whitebark pine tree that showed signs of mountain pine beetle infestation. The average number of live whitebark pine trees per plot was 94 (±106 [SD]), with a maximum of 299 trees in a single densely populated krummholz stand. Approximately 18% of live whitebark pine trees produced female cones. Clark's nutcrackers (*Nucifraga columbiana*) were detected in 7 of the 11 plots, but no detections of Douglas squirrels (*Tamiasciurus douglasii*) were made.

In the SEKI foxtail pine plots, 225 live foxtail pine trees and 86 whitebark pine trees were measured and tagged. Thirty-one dead trees unassigned to species were also recorded. No signs of blister rust infection or mountain pine beetle infestation were found. The average number of foxtail pine trees per plot was 32 (±19 [SD]), with a maximum of 62 trees counted in one plot. No foxtail seedlings and saplings were recorded within the regeneration plots. Two whitebark pine seedlings and one whitebark pine sapling were recorded in the single plot containing both species. Sixty percent of the foxtail pine trees produced female cones in 2011. Clark's nutcrackers were detected in 2 of the 7 foxtail pine plots. Douglas squirrels were undetected in all 7 plots.

Based on this first season of implementation, we made minor adjustments to the monitoring protocol, which has recently been approved through a peer-review process and published (McKinney et al. 2012a and 2012b). The changes primarily pertained to plot orientation and subplot sampling order. Panel 1 plots not established in 2011 will be established during the first revisit cycle, which is projected to be 2015. As a result of the field crew's serious accident, the Sierra Nevada Network I&M Program has reviewed and improved its safety program, included more safety-related guidance and tools in seasonal training sessions, and refined our field communication procedures.

Acknowledgments

Funding for this project was provided through the National Park Service Natural Resource Challenge and the Servicewide Inventory and Monitoring Program. We thank the Park superintendents and resource staff who met with us to discuss park management objectives and information needs, and who provided invaluable logistical support to field operations in 2011. Tom Rodhouse provided helpful comments during the preparation of this report. Adrian Das, Tony Caprio, and Alice Chung-MacCoubrey provided insightful reviews of the report that improved its content and clarity. We also thank Dan Esposito, Matt Nolte, and Jim Syvertsen for their efforts in gathering the data presented in this publication.

Background and Objectives

Many western North American coniferous forests are currently facing unprecedented health challenges, including upsurges of native pests and pathogens, invasive exotic species, and altered disturbance regimes. Increased atmospheric warming, carbon dioxide concentration, and nitrogen deposition, as well as changes in precipitation patterns (i.e., timing, magnitude, and type) pose additional short- and long-term threats. Each factor alone can alter forest ecosystem structure, function, and species composition, and additive or synergistic effects are likely if multiple agents act jointly. How forest ecosystems will respond to modern perturbations is uncertain. However the magnitude of change in structure and composition, and key ecological processes will likely be exceptional. Indeed, increased tree mortality rates over the last several decades have recently been documented across a broad range of latitude and forest types in western North America (van Mantgem et al. 2009), which may have important consequences for forest stand dynamics and ecosystem functions.

Five-needle white pines (Family Pinaceae, Genus *Pinus*, Subgenus *Strobus*), and in particular whitebark pine (*Pinus albicaulis*), limber pine (*P. flexilis*), and foxtail pine (*P. balfouriana*) are foundational species (Tomback and Achuff 2010) in upper subalpine and treeline forests of several National Park Service (NPS) Pacific West Region (PWR) parks, including Sequoia and Kings Canyon National Parks (SEKI) and Yosemite National Park (YOSE). Ongoing declines of many foundation tree species pose an especially compelling problem because these species provide fundamental structure to a system and are thereby irreplaceable (Ellison et al. 2005). Foundation species generally occupy low trophic levels, create locally stable conditions required by many other species, and stabilize fundamental ecosystem processes (Ellison et al. 2005). In temperate zone forests (e.g., western North America) there often are only one or two foundational tree species, and therefore little functional redundancy is present in the system. If a foundation tree species is lost from these systems, it will likely lead to a cascade of secondary losses, shifts in biological diversity, and ultimately affect the functioning and stability of the community (Ebenman and Jonsson 2005).

Whitebark Pine

Whitebark pine occurs across a broad geographic range, reaching its southern limit in central California in the Mount Whitney vicinity and occurs on both the west and the more arid east side of the Sierra Nevada crest. Throughout its range, whitebark pine can occur in the montane, upper subalpine, and treeline zones (Arno and Hoff 1990; 1,370–3,660 m above sea level rangewide). It occurs as the only tree species on the coldest and driest sites near treeline and as a seral species on protected, slightly lower sites more favorable to its shade-tolerant competitors (Arno and Weaver 1990).

In the Pacific West region, whitebark pine is scattered across tens of thousands of hectares in the high elevations of SEKI and YOSE (Figure 1). White pine blister rust (*Cronartium ribicola*) infections on whitebark pine decrease from north to south in the Pacific West region, resembling the trend seen in the Rocky Mountains. Blister rust is relatively rare in SEKI and YOSE when compared to regions within the UCBN. Mountain pine beetles (*Dendroctonus ponderosae*) are currently abundant in the northern Cascades, but also decrease with latitude (Gibson et al. 2008) in the Pacific West region.

1

Whitebark pine acts as a foundation species in high-elevation forest communities by regulating ecosystem processes, community composition and dynamics, and by influencing regional biodiversity (Ellison et al. 2005, Tomback and Kendall 2001). Whitebark pine plays a role in initiating community development after fire, influencing snowmelt and stream flow, and preventing soil erosion at high elevations (Tomback et al. 2001, Farnes 1990). The large, wingless seeds of whitebark pine are high in fat, carbohydrates, and lipids and provide an important food source for many granivorous birds and mammals (Tomback and Kendall 2001). Whitebark pine is a coevolved mutualist with Clark's nutcracker (*Nucifraga columbiana*), and is dependent upon nutcrackers for dispersal of its large, wingless seeds (Tomback 1982). Nutcrackers are a facultative mutualist; they favor whitebark pine seeds, but also disperse seeds of other large-seeded conifers (e.g., ponderosa pine [*P. ponderosa*]). Nutcrackers extract seeds from indehiscent cones in late summer and early fall and often cache seeds in recently disturbed sites, accounting for the whitebark pine's early successional status. Whitebark pine also provides important habitat structure for high-elevation vertebrates.

Foxtail Pine
Foxtail pine is endemic to two distinct areas in California, the Klamath Mountains in the northwest part of the state and the southern Sierra Nevada (Figure 1). Research on community and population dynamics is lacking for foxtail pine compared to whitebark pine. Foxtail pine occurs in four different forest types: 1) stands dominated by foxtail pine, 2) stands with foxtail pine and whitebark pine, 3) stands with foxtail pine and red fir (*Abies magnifica*), and 4) stands with foxtail pine, red fir, and western white pine (*P. monticola*) (Eckert and Sawyer 2002). Foxtail and whitebark pine overlap in some portions of their southern Sierra Nevada distribution, however, in many areas of the southern Sierra Nevada, foxtail pine is the major (exclusive) subalpine and treeline tree species (e.g., >3,000 m). Foxtail pine provides important habitat and food resources for birds and mammals, and influences snow melt and soil erosion. Foxtail pine seeds are wind dispersed. However, nutcrackers are known to harvest seeds from foxtail cones of the previous year and have been observed caching seeds of unknown species within foxtail pine stands (S. T. McKinney, personal observation). It is also currently unknown whether seed caching rodents play a role in foxtail pine seedling establishment.

The southern population of foxtail, subspecies *austrina*, provides important data for dendrochronological research on paleoclimate (Lloyd 1997) as a consequence of its great longevity (> 1,000 years) and slow growth. In fact five-needle pines, in general, have proven valuable in enhancing our understanding of past climates through dendrochronological investigations (e.g., Kipfmueller and Salzer 2010, Woodhouse et al. 2011).

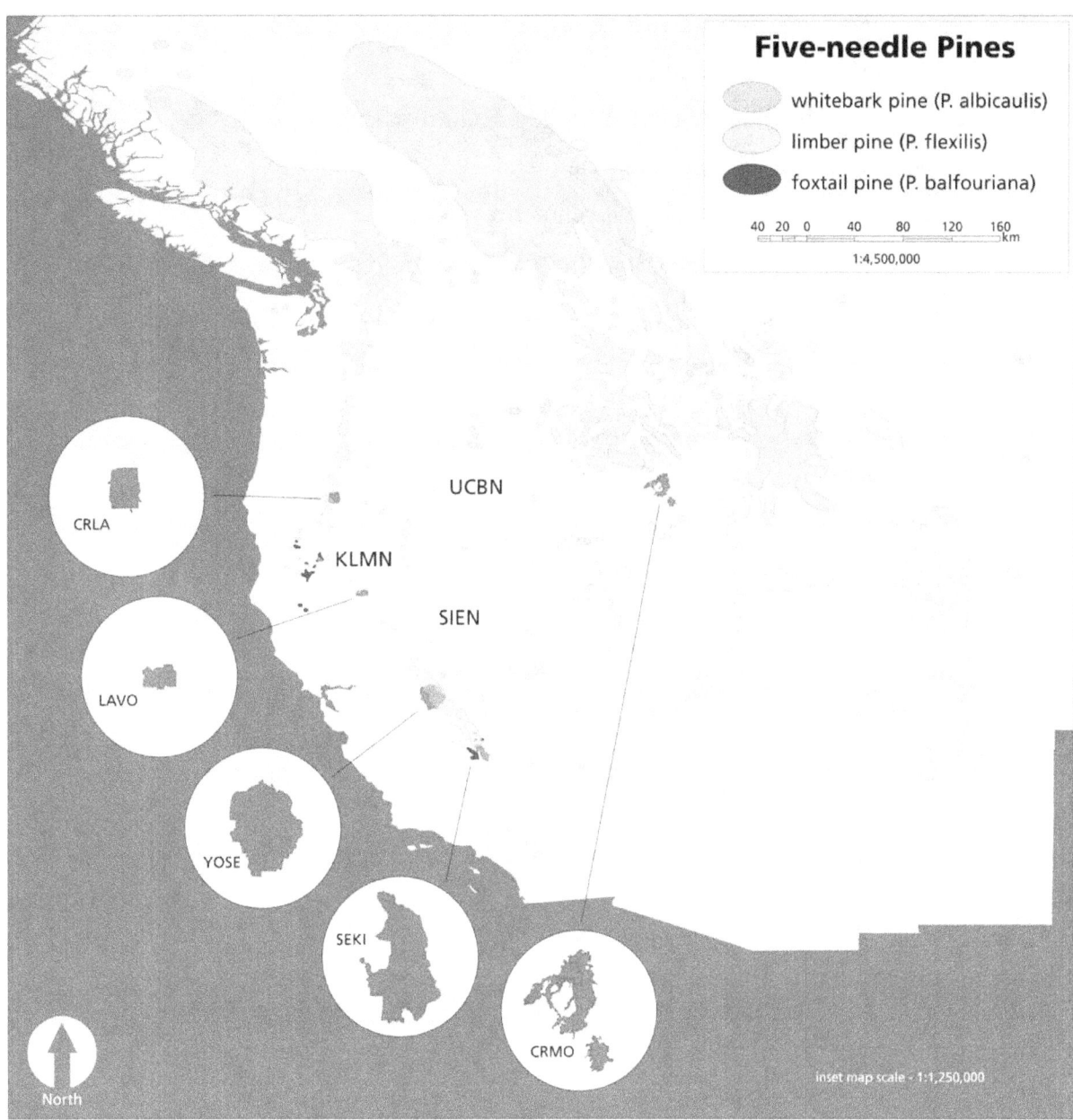

Figure 1. Distribution of whitebark pine, limber pine, and foxtail pine (from Little 1971) and locations of three Pacific West Region networks and associated parks.

Objectives

Monitoring objectives were established through a collaborative process with ecologists from KLMN, SIEN, and the UCBN as part of a multi-network white pine monitoring protocol (McKinney et al. 2012a). The objectives were also linked to the vital signs that were developed by each network and documented in network monitoring plans (Garrett et al. 2007, Sarr et al. 2007, Mutch et al. 2008). The anticipated impacts from blister rust, dwarf mistletoe, mountain pine beetle, and climate change on high-elevation pines based on published results and expert opinion were also driving factors in determining objectives. Through an approach that involves monitoring individual trees within permanent plots, key demographic parameters within white pine forest communities will be estimated. The objectives are to detect status and trend in:

1. Trees species composition and structure
2. Tree species birth, death, and growth rates
3. Incidence of white pine blister rust and level of crown kill
4. Incidence of pine beetle and level of crown kill
5. Incidence of dwarf mistletoe and level of crown kill
6. Cone production of white pine species

Ancillary data on habitat use of white pine communities by Clark's nutcrackers and Douglas squirrels were also collected in SEKI and YOSE in 2011.

Methods

This section provides a detailed summary of the methods used for white pine monitoring in SEKI and YOSE. For the complete methodology of white pine monitoring, refer to the collaborative white pine monitoring protocol for networks in the Pacific West Region (McKinney et al. 2012a, 2012b)

Sampling Frame

White pine monitoring plots and sampling frames were established within appropriate plant associations throughout SEKI and YOSE. The YOSE and SEKI vegetation maps identified the distribution of whitebark and foxtail pine and were used to define individual sampling frames for each species-park population (Figures 2 – 4). For all three sampling frames, areas with a slope greater than 35 degrees were excluded due to safety considerations. Scope of inference extends broadly across mapped stands of YOSE and SEKI, limited only by the slope cutoff.

The sites to be sampled were identified using a randomized spatially-balanced sampling design via the Generalized Random Tessellation Stratified (GRTS) algorithm (Stevens and Olsen 2004). This design assigns permanent plots to random locations within the sampling frame while keeping the order of plots sampled unstructured, of equal-probability, and spatially balanced. This method allows for the addition of new sites or replacement sites which is useful in eliminating sampling difficulties that arise from site inaccessibility or sampling frame errors where, for instance, an unsuitable habitat type was erroneously mapped as suitable.

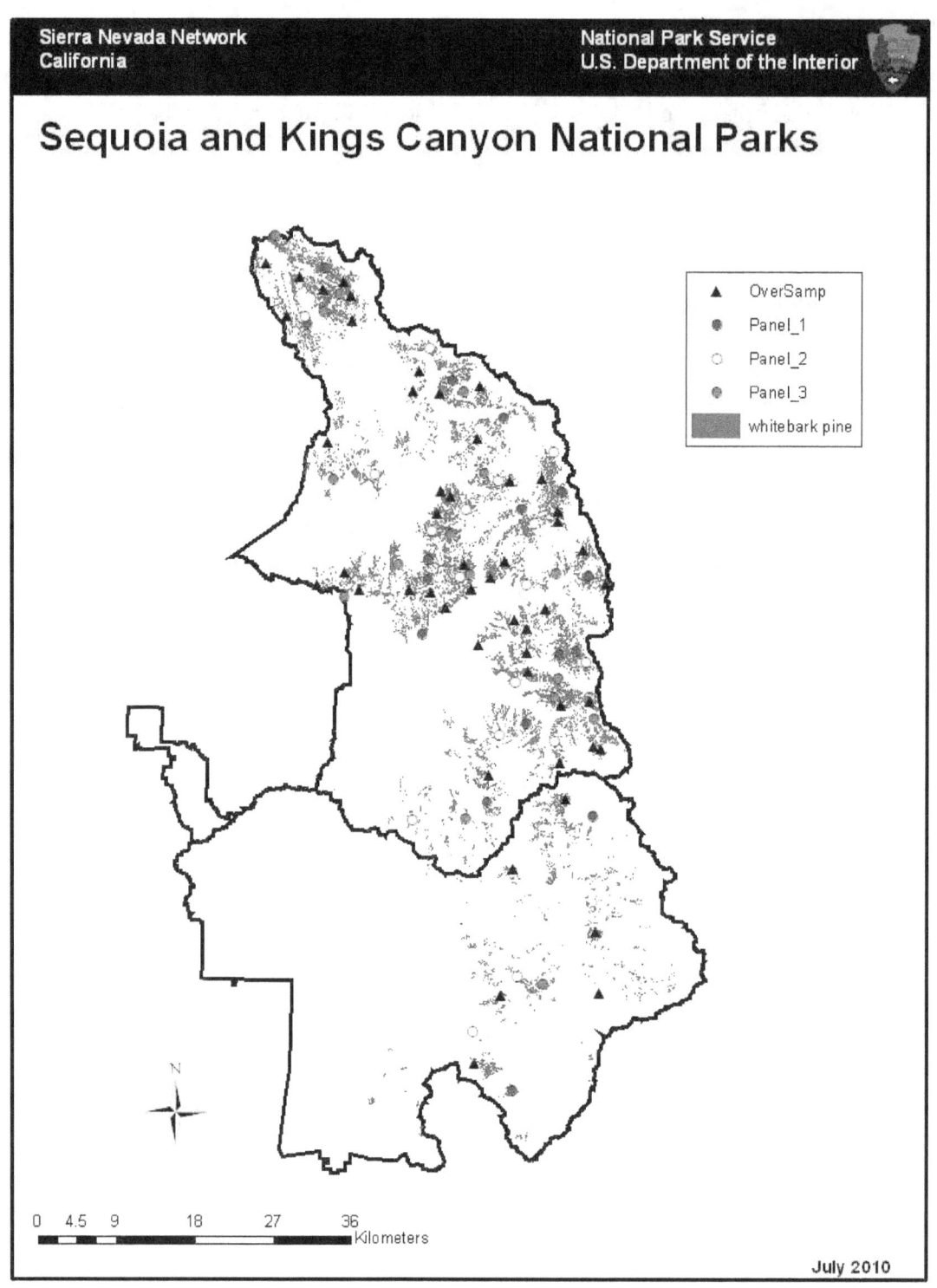

Figure 2. Whitebark pine sampling frame (green, sampling frame equals known population) and GRTS sample of plot locations for Sequoia and Kings Canyon National Parks. Sample locations are separated into 3 equal panels of 16 plots each. Each plot will be sampled once every 3 years in a rotating panel sampling design. An oversample of points was also drawn using the GRTS algorithm to support any eventual site additions, deletions, or replacements.

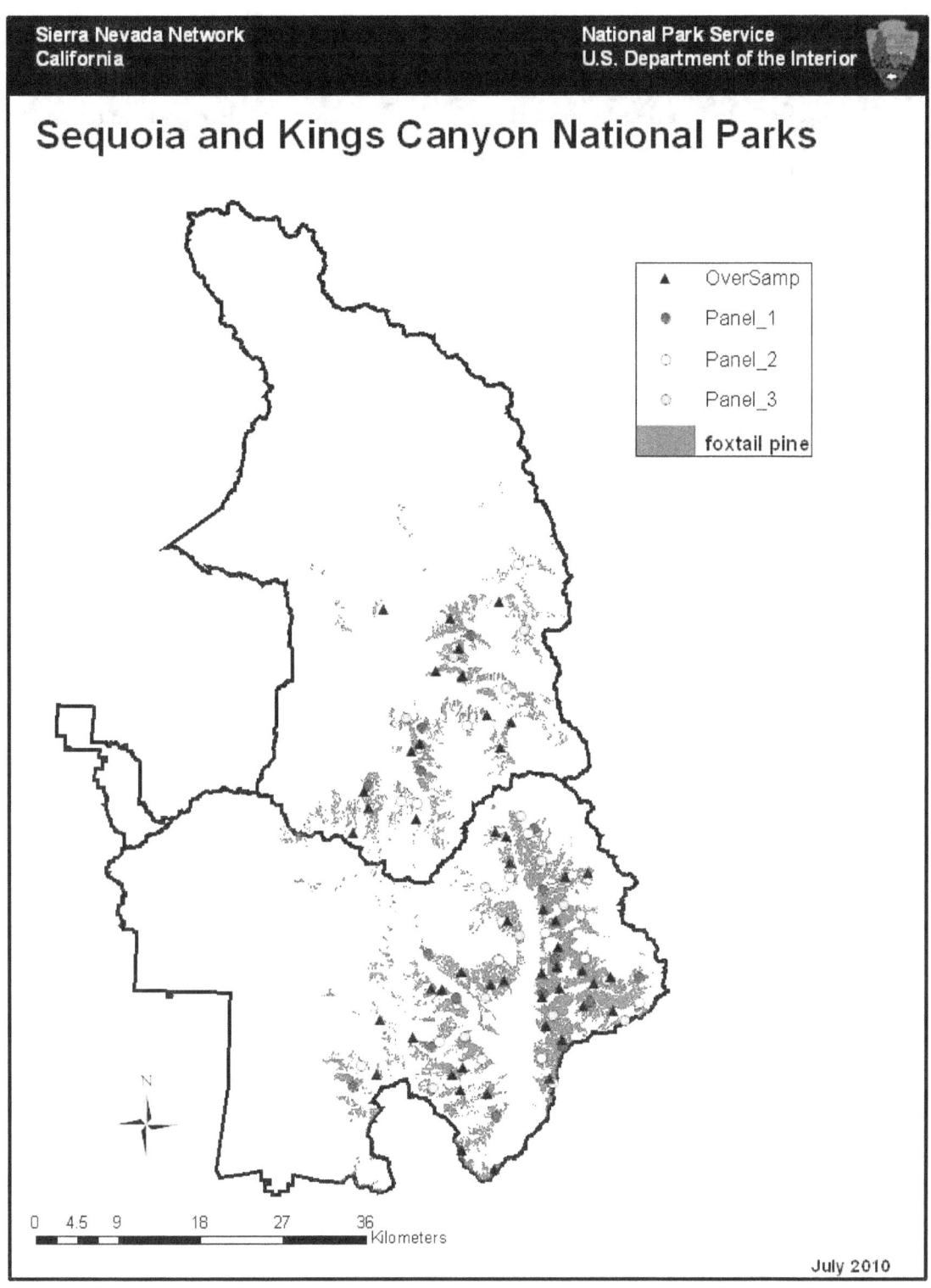

Figure 3. Foxtail pine sampling frame (red, sampling frame equals known population) and GRTS sample of plot locations for Sequoia and Kings Canyon National Parks. Sample locations are separated into 3 equal panels of 16 plots each. Each plot will be sampled once every 3 years in a rotating panel sampling design. An oversample of points was also drawn using the GRTS algorithm to support any eventual site additions, deletions, or replacements.

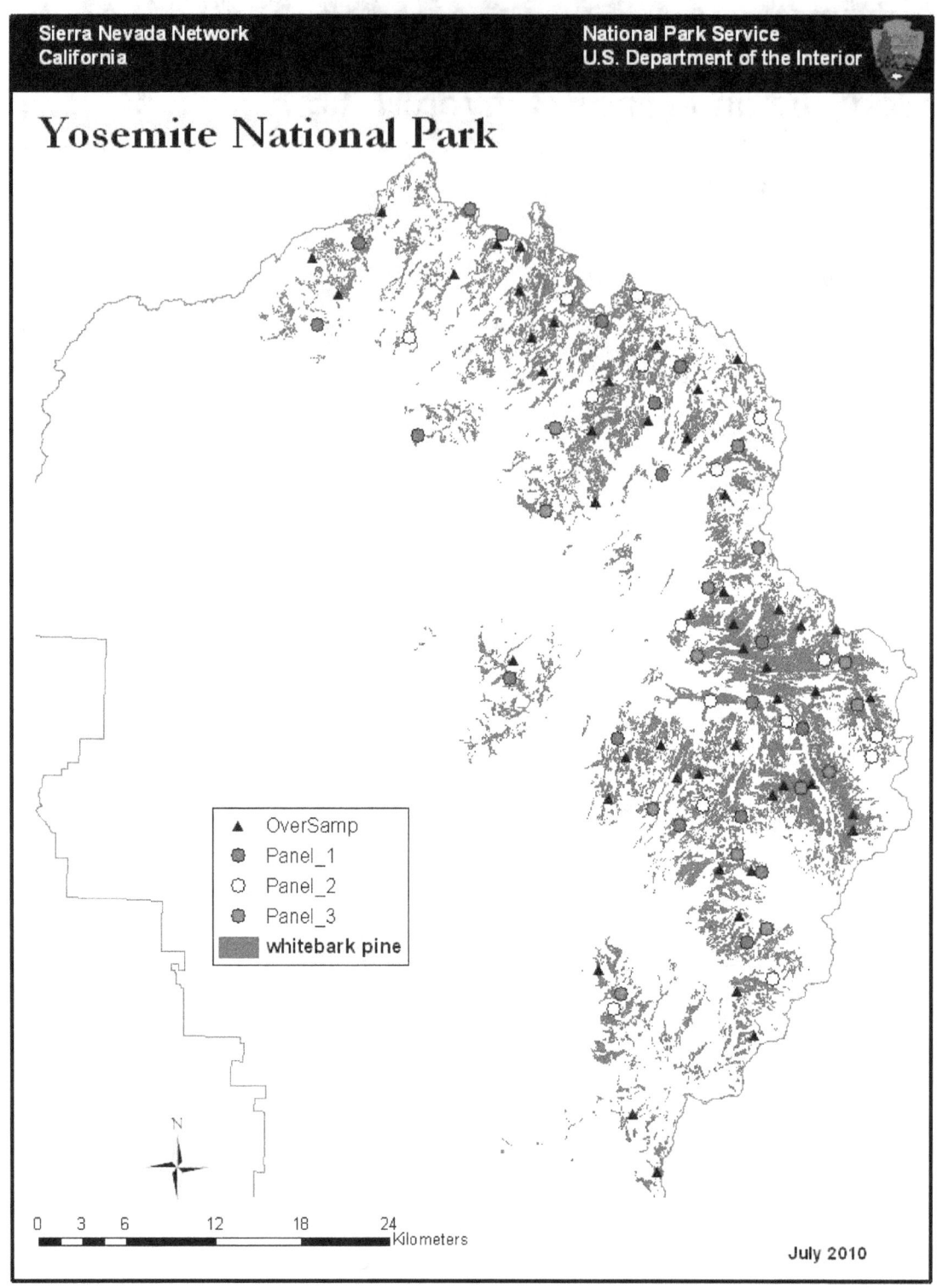

Figure 4. Whitebark pine sampling frame (green, sampling frame equals known population) and GRTS sample of plot locations for Yosemite National Park. Sample locations are separated into three equal panels of 16 plots each. Each plot will be sampled once every three years in a rotating panel sampling design. An oversample of points was also drawn using the GRTS algorithm to support any eventual site additions, deletions, or replacements.

Frequency and Timing of Sampling

We adopted a three-year rotating panel design for re-surveying permanent plots in SEKI and YOSE. Sampling will occur between June and October and each plot will be surveyed once per 3-year rotation (a [1-2^3] design, McDonald 2003) (Table 1). A total of 48 plots will be monitored in each park (YOSE and SEKI) for each species, resulting in an overall total sampling effort of 96 plots in SEKI (48 whitebark and 48 foxtail) and 48 plots in YOSE (whitebark only).

Table 1. Revisit design for monitoring white pine species in the Sierra Nevada Network. This panel design is followed for whitebark pine in YOSE and whitebark and foxtail pine each in SEKI for a total SIEN n = 144plots.

Panel	Year												
	2011	2012	2013	2014	2015	2016	2017	2018	2019	2020	2021	2022	2023
1 (n = 16)	x			x			x			x			x
2 (n = 16)		x			x			x			x		
3 (n = 16)			x			x			x			x	

Plot Layout

Macroplots, consisting of 5 subplots and containing 9 seedling/sapling regeneration plots are used to measure and track forest demographic parameters, disease and insect occurrence, and magnitude of their impact (Figure 5). The response design for this protocol is compatible with the *Interagency Whitebark Pine Monitoring Protocol for the Greater Yellowstone Ecosystem* (GYWPMWG 2007) but differs in some respects, most notably, plot size. The 10 x 50 m plot size from the Yellowstone protocol has been increased to accommodate the often sparse distribution of white pines in our PWR parks and to adequately address forest demographic objectives. Following analyses of pilot data collected in network parks in 2009–2010, the SIEN decided to use a 50 x 50 m plot (0.25 ha or 2,500 m^2) (McKinney et al. 2012a). This design effectively represents five parallel 10 x 50 m subplots as used in the GRYN and as proposed by the Whitebark Pine Ecosystem Foundation (Tomback et al. 2005).

A total of nine square regeneration plots (3 x 3 m) are established within each 50 x 50 m macroplot to measure seedling regeneration (Figure 5). Regeneration plots are located at each corner (4), at each midpoint between corners (4), and in the middle (1) of the macroplot (Figure 5). The current design was chosen because it provides a reasonable balance among sampling time constraints, observer accuracy and precision, and total area sampled.

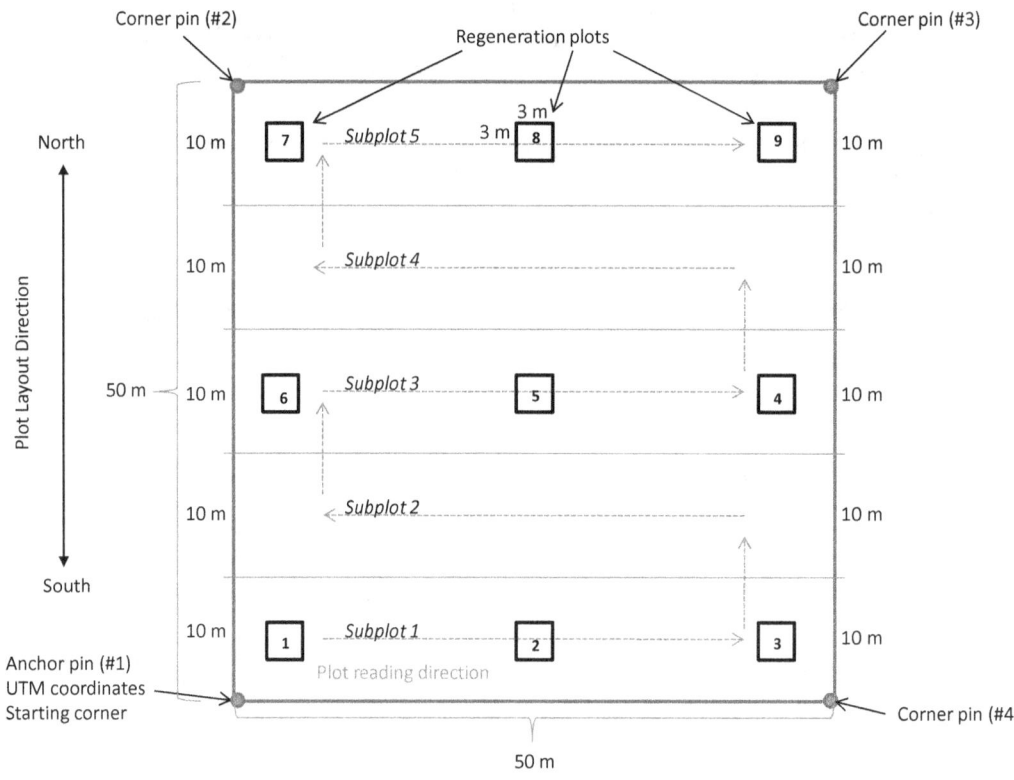

Figure 5. 50 x 50 m permanent plot layout used in SIEN white pine monitoring.

Plot Measurements

Table 2 outlines the relationship among the variables, raw data, summarized data, and monitoring objectives. Detailed instructions on response design measurements are provided by McKinney et al. (2012a, 2012b) and only a general overview is presented here.

Each live tree taller than 1.37 m has a uniquely numbered metal tag attached to it, its species identified, and diameter at 1.37 m (breast height, dbh) and tree height measured. Dead trees are tagged and are recorded as either recently dead or dead. Recently dead trees have red needles present (but no green needles) and dead trees have no needles present. White pine blister rust infection is assessed for all living white pine trees. The bole and branches of white pine trees are each vertically divided into thirds (upper, middle, and bottom) and each third is assigned one of three rust condition classes: 1) absent–no sign of rust infection, 2) active cankers (aeciospores present), or 3) no active cankers, but with the presence of at least three of the following five indicators of infection: rodent chewing, flagging, swelling, roughened bark, and oozing sap. Mountain pine beetle occurrence is recorded for all pine trees using three indicators of beetle activity: pitch tubes, frass, and J-shaped galleries. The presence of galleries is only determined for recently dead and dead trees because bark has to be removed for this assessment. Current dwarf mistletoe infection is recorded for all living white pine trees by noting presence or absence of mistletoe for each third of a tree, similar to the Hawksworth rating system (1977). The level of canopy kill in live white pine trees afflicted with one of the three previously mentioned stressors is determined by dividing the tree's canopy (all the main branches, encompassing all foliage and supporting twigs and side branches) into thirds and ocularly estimating the percentage of each third of the canopy that is dead. Cone production is recorded as to whether female cones are present or absent on each white pine tree. Live seedlings are tallied by species and height class in regeneration plots. Height classes are 1) 20 to <50 cm, 2) 50 to <100 cm, and 3) 100 to <137 cm. Seedlings <20 cm are not measured.

Table 2. Relationship among variables, data, and objectives, from McKinney et al. (*2012a*).

Variable	Raw Data	Summarized Data	Objectives Addressed
Species	Tree (nominal)	Trees per hectare (TPH); all spp., each spp., proportion of total by spp.	1. composition & structure
Diameter	Tree (cm)	Basal area (m^2/ha); all spp., each spp., proportion of total by spp. Mean diameter (cm) by spp. Diameter classes (5 cm); proportion and TPH by spp.	1. composition & structure 2. growth rate
Height	Tree (m)	Mean ht. (m); all spp. and by each spp. Height classes (3 m); proportion and TPH by spp.	1. composition & structure 2. growth rate
Status	Tree (live or dead)	Proportion live and dead; all spp and by each sp. TPH and proportion by 5 cm diameter classes in each condition; all spp and by each sp.	2. birth and death rates
Crown kill	Each of three parts of a tree (%)	Mean (%); individual trees, each sp, and all spp.	3. level of crown kill
Active canker	Each of three parts of a tree (p/a)	Proportion and TPH with active cankers by each white pine sp.	3. rust infection incidence
Inactive blister rust canker	Each of three parts of a tree (p/a)	Proportion and TPH with inactive cankers by each white pine sp.	3. rust infection incidence
Rust infection	Tree (p/a of active or inactive canker)	Proportion and TPH infected and healthy by each white pine sp. TPH by 5 cm diameter classes in each condition by each white pine sp.	3. rust infection incidence
Bark beetle	Tree (p/a)	Proportion and TPH with beetle sign; all spp and each sp.	4. incidence of bark beetle
Dwarf mistletoe	Tree (p/a)	Proportion and TPH with mistletoe sign; all spp and each sp.	5. incidence of dwarf mistletoe
Female cones	Tree (p/a)	Proportion and TPH with cones by each white pine sp.	6. cone production
Seedlings	9 m^2 plot; number of each of three size classes by species	Mean (number per m^2); all spp and each sp for each size class.	1. composition & structure 2. birth rates

2011 Sampling Logistics

A four person crew was hired to establish and sample up to 48 plots within YOSE and SEKI during the 2011 field season. The crew was composed of two seasonal biological science technicians from SIEN and two from UCBN. Supervisory responsibilities of the crew were shared between the project leads for each network. Due to logistical and budget constraints, our 2011 field season objectives were to establish 11 of the 16 plots for each species-park population (33 plots total), with the remaining plots being installed on the first revisit to panel 1 in 2015. Training occurred over a one week period in June at CRMO, was led by the UCBN and SIEN project leads, and included training on forest pathology by experts from the U.S. Forest Service. The crew began plot installation and sampling at CRMO in July before traveling to YOSE and SEKI.

Results and Discussion

YOSE

Summary statistics for the YOSE whitebark pine plots are provided in Table 3. From July 25 to August 18, 2011, 11 plots were established throughout whitebark pine stands in YOSE. These plots contained a total of 1745 trees: 1,039 whitebark pine trees (1 dead), 382 lodgepole pine trees (2 dead, 5 recently dead), 270 mountain hemlock trees (*Tsuga mertensiana*; 8 dead), 31 western juniper trees (*Juniperus occidentalis*), three Jeffrey pine trees (*P. jeffreyi*), and 20 dead trees that were not identified to species. For the 1,038 live whitebark pine trees, 31 % displayed a krummholtz growth form and the average number of stems per clump was 3.4[1] (range = 2 to 11). No indication of white pine blister rust or dwarf mistletoe was found within the 11 established plots in YOSE, but there was one live whitebark pine tree that showed signs of mountain pine beetle infestation. The average number of whitebark pine trees per plot (2500 m^2) was 94 with a range of 6 to 299 trees in a densely populated krummholz stand. Approximately 18% of live whitebark pine trees (*n* = 190) produced female cones. Clark's nutcrackers were detected in 7 of 11 of plots, but no indication of Douglas squirrel use was found.

Table 3. Summary statistics on whitebark pine plots installed at YOSE in 2011 (n = 11).

	Average (SD)	Range
P. albicaulis density (trees/ha)	377 (423)	24 - 1196
Other species density (trees/ha)	244 (278)	0 - 732
Snag density (dead trees/ha)	8 (9)	0 - 56
P. albicaulis average dbh (cm)	7.1 (3.8)	3.7 - 15.8
Other species average dbh (cm)	20.2 (10.2)	4.2 - 34.2
Snag average dbh (dead tree cm)	25.2 (11.8)	9.5 - 42.4
P. albicaulis Basal Area (m^2/ha)	2.7 (4.1)	0.1 - 12.2
Other species Basal Area (m^2/ha)	20.5 (25.5)	0 - 59.7
Snag Basal Area (dead tree m^2/ha)	1.0 (1.4)	0 - 4.4
P. albicaulis blister rust infection rate (# of infected trees/ha)	0	0
Dwarf mistletoe infection rate (# of infected trees/ha)	0	0
Mountain pine beetle infestation rate (# of infested trees/ha)	0.4	0 - 4
P. albicaulis seedling regeneration 20-136 cm (seedlings/ha)	819 (1598)	0 - 4444
Other species seedling regeneration 20-136 cm (seedlings/ha)	393 (1028)	0 - 3457
P. albicaulis female cone production (# of trees with cones/ha)	69 (109)	0 - 292

SEKI

From August 24 to September 8, 2011, we installed and sampled seven plots in the SEKI-foxtail pine population. Summary statistics are provided in Table 4. These plots contained a total of 225 foxtail pine trees, 101 lodgepole trees (1 recently dead), and 86 whitebark pine trees. The whitebark trees all occurred within one plot. There were also 31 dead trees of unidentified species. Of the 225 foxtail pines, 8 % displayed a krummholtz growth form and the average number of trees per clump was 2.0[1]. For whitebark pine, 22 % displayed a krummholtz growth form and the average number of trees per clump was 2.4[1]. No foxtail or whitebark pine trees were found to have signs of blister rust infection, mountain pine beetle, or dwarf mistletoe within the sampling areas. The average number of white pines per plot was 44 (32 foxtail, 12 whitebark) with a range of 1 to 148. There were no foxtail seedlings or saplings recorded in the regeneration

---

[1] These numbers likely overestimate the percentage of krummholtz trees as it includes all trees that shared a base.

plots, but 2 whitebark pine seedlings (20-50 cm) and 1 whitebark pine sapling (100-136 cm) were recorded in the plot containing both white pine species. Sixty percent of the foxtail pine trees (*n* = 135) produced female cones in 2011. Clark's nutcrackers were detected in 2 of 7 plots, but no indication of Douglas squirrel use was found in any plot.

During the 2011 field season, only seven plots were established because of a serious injury to a member of the crew which occurred on September 8. Due to the accident severity, we ended the field season early and were thus unable to complete the foxtail pine plots or establish any whitebark pine plots at SEKI. The additional 9 foxtail plots and 16 whitebark pine plots that were not established in 2011 will be installed during the first panel 1 re-measure scheduled for 2015.

Table 4. Summary statistics on foxtail pine plots installed at SEKI in 2011 (n = 7).

	Average (SD)	Range
P. balfouriana density (trees/ha)	129 (75)	4 - 248
Other *species* density (trees/ha)	106 (142)	0 - 372
Snag density (dead trees/ha)	18 (15)	0 - 44
P. balfouriana average dbh (cm)	35.5 (17.4)	12.6 - 57.4
Other species average dbh (cm)	30.3 (15.0)	7.6 - 45.2
Snag average dbh (dead tree cm)	38.9 (16.7)	8.2 - 53.9
P. balfouriana Basal Area (m^2/ha)	22.0 (16.3)	0.1 - 44.2
Other species Basal Area (m^2/ha)	7.7 (14.4)	0 - 40.1
Snag Basal Area (dead tree m^2/ha)	3.0 (2.6)	0 - 6.0
P. balfouriana blister rust infection rate (# of infected trees/ha)	0	0
Dwarf mistletoe infection rate (# of infected trees/ha)	0	0
Mountain pine beetle infestation rate (# of infested trees/ha)	0	0
P. balfouriana seedling regeneration 20-136 cm (seedlings/ha)	0	0
Other species seedling regeneration 20-136 cm (seedlings/ha)	71 (140)	0 - 370
P. balfouriana female cone production (# of trees with cones/ha)	77 (48)	4 - 124

Summary

Results of this first year of data collection indicate that the forested area sampled within SEKI and YOSE currently have a very low incidence of white pine blister rust, dwarf mistletoe, and mountain pine beetle. These results are consistent with the limited data known for the Sierra Nevada region (Duriscoe and Duriscoe 2002) and contrast sharply with whitebark pine health conditions in the Cascade and Rocky Mountain regions. Whitebark pine and foxtail pine occur near their southern-most geographic limit in SEKI. Results from the SIEN monitoring project may prove particularly relevant to forecasting population trajectories for the two species in the face of rapid regional warming (Diaz & Eischeid 2007). Understanding the dynamics of whitebark and foxtail pine populations in this region could provide answers to how the species may respond to drought and other climatic events projected to occur with greater frequency and severity over the next century. Information gathered from this white pine monitoring project will be integral to providing a more comprehensive understanding of the populations within SIEN parks as well as providing for comparisons across broader geographic areas. It will also allow early detection of important changes in populations that may require management intervention. This information will be particularly powerful if incorporated into an adaptive management framework, where it can be used to formulate sound, science-based management decisions at the park-level.

Suggested/Required Changes to the Protocol

Based on this first season of monitoring, only minor changes to the protocol were made which were primarily concerned with the position of the plot, the position of regeneration plots within, and the diagram of these plots (Figure 5 in this document). Plot orientation, which was originally arranged to be aligned upslope with the origin on the downhill side, has been changed so that the plot is aligned along the cardinal directions and with the plot origin now being the southwest corner and the subplots running east and west. This change was made to standardize the way that plots were oriented and to avoid confusion during plot setup in the field. Another change was made to the order of regeneration plot surveys. The numbers of the 4th and 6th regeneration plots have been reversed to facilitate more efficient sampling. Lastly, the plot layout figure (Figure 5) has been updated to address these changes. These changes were incorporated prior to final approval of the protocol (McKinney et al. 2012a, 2012b

Literature Cited

Arno, S. F., and T. Weaver. 1990. Whitebark pine community types and their patterns on the landscape. Pages 97-105 *in* W. C. Schmidt and K. J. McDonald, editors. Proceedings of the Symposium on whitebark pine ecosystems: ecology and management of a high-elevation resource. USDA Forest Service General Technical Report INT-GTR-270. USDA Forest Service, Rocky Mountain Research Station, Fort Collins, Colorado.

Arno, S. F.; and R. J. Hoff. 1990. *Pinus albicaulis* Engelm. Whitebark pine. Pages 268-279 *in* R. P. Burns and B. H. Honkala, editors. Silvics of North America, Volume 1, Conifers. Agriculture Handbook 654. USDA Forest Service, Washington, D.C.

Diaz, H. F. and J. K. Eischeid. 2007. Disappearing "alpine tundra" Köppen climatic type in the western United States. Geophysical Research Letters, 34, L18707 doi:10.1029/2007GL031253

Duriscoe, D. M. and C. S. Duriscoe. 2002. Survey and monitoring of white pine blister rust in Sequoia and Kings Canyon National Parks—Final report of 1995-1999 survey and monitoring plot network. Science and Natural Resources Management Division, Sequoia and Kings Canyon National Parks.

Ebenman, B., and T. Jonsson. 2005. Using community viability analysis to identify fragile systems and keystone species. Trends in Ecology and Evolution 20:568–575.

Eckert, A. J., and J. O. Sawyer. 2002. Foxtail pine importance and conifer diversity in the Klamath Mountains and southern Sierra Nevada, California. Madroño 49:33-45.

Ellison, A. E., M. S. Bank, B. D. Clinton, E. A. Colburn, K. Elliott, C. R. Ford, D. R. Foster, B. D. Kloeppel, J. D. Knoepp, G. M. Lovett, and others. 2005. Loss of foundation species: consequences for the structure and dynamics of forested ecosystems. Frontiers in Ecology and the Environment 3:479–486.

Farnes, P. E. 1990. SNOTEL and snow course data describing the hydrology of whitebark pine ecosystems. Pages 302–304 *in* W. C. Schmidt and K. J. McDonald, editors. Proceedings of the Symposium on whitebark pine ecosystems: ecology and management of a high-elevation resource, 29–31 March 1989, Bozeman, Montana. USDA Forest Service General Technical Report INT-GTR-270. USDA Forest Service, Rocky Mountain Research Station, Fort Collins, Colorado.

Garrett, L. K., T. J. Rodhouse, G. H. Dicus, C. C. Caudill, and M. R. Shardlow. 2007. Upper Columbia Basin Network vital signs monitoring plan. Natural Resource Report NPS/ UCBN/NRR—2007/002. National Park Service, Fort Collins, Colorado.

Gibson, K., K. Skov, S. Kegley, C. Jorgensen, S. Smith, and J. Witcosky. 2008. Mountain pine beetle impacts in high-elevation five-needle pines: Current trends and challenges. U.S. Department of Agriculture, Forest Service, Forest Health Protection Report R1-08-020.

Greater Yellowstone Whitebark Pine Monitoring Working Group. 2007. Interagency whitebark pine monitoring protocol for the Greater Yellowstone Ecosystem, v 1.0. Greater Yellowstone Coordinating Committee, Bozeman, Montana. Unpublished.

Hawksworth, Frank G. 1977. The 6-class dwarf mistletoe rating system. General Technical Report RM-48. USDA Forest Service Rocky Mountain Forest and Range Experiment Station, Fort Collins, CO. 7p.

Kipfmueller, K. F., and M. W. Salzer. 2010. Linear trend and climate response of five-needle pines in the western United States related to treeline proximity. Canadian Journal of Forest Research 40: 134-142.

Lloyd, A. H. 1997. Response of tree-line populations of foxtail pine (*Pinus balfouriana*) to climate variation over the last 1000 years. Canadian Journal of Forest Research 27:936-942.

McDonald, T. L. 2003. Review of environmental monitoring methods: Survey designs. Environmental Monitoring and Assessment 85:277–292.

McKinney, S. T., T. Rodhouse, L. Chow, A. Chung-MacCoubrey, G. Dicus, L. Garrett, K. Irvine, S. Mohren, D. Odion, D. Sarr, and L. A. Starcevich. 2012a. Monitoring white pine (*Pinus albicaulis, P. balfouriana, P. flexilis*) community dynamics in the Pacific West Region - Klamath, Sierra Nevada, and Upper Columbia Basin Networks: Narrative version 1.0. Natural Resource Report NPS/PWR/ NRR—2012/532. National Park Service, Fort Collins, Colorado.

McKinney, S. T., T. Rodhouse, L. Chow, A. Chung-MacCoubrey, G. Dicus, L. Garrett, K. Irvine, S. Mohren, D. Odion, D. Sarr, and L. A. Starcevich. 2012b. Monitoring white pine (Pinus albicaulis, P. balfouriana, P. flexilis) community dynamics in the Pacific West Region - Klamath, Sierra Nevada, and Upper Columbia Basin Networks: Standard operating procedures version 1.0 (Appendix A to Narrative Version 1.0). Natural Resource Report NPS/PWR/NRR—2012/533. National Park Service, Fort Collins, Colorado.

Millar, C. I., R. D. Westfall, D. L. Delany, M. J. Bokach, A. L. Flint, and L. E. Flint. 2012. Forest mortality in high-elevation whitebark pine (*Pinus albicaulis*) forests of eastern California, USA; influence of environmental context, bark beetles, climatic water decicit, and warming. Canadian Journal of Forest Research 42: 749-765.

Mutch, L. S., M. G. Rose, A. M. Heard, R. R. Cook, and G. L. Entsminger. 2008. Sierra Nevada Network vital signs monitoring plan. Natural Resource Report NPS/ SIEN/NRR—2008/072. National Park Service, Fort Collins, Colorado.

Sarr, D. A., D. C. Odion, S. R. Mohren, E. E. Perry, R. L. Hoffman, L. K. Bridy, and A. A. Merton. 2007. Vital signs monitoring plan for the Klamath Network: Phase III report. Natural Resource Technical Report NPS/KLMN/NRR—2007/016, National Park Service, Fort Collins, Colorado.

Stevens, D. L., and A. R. Olsen. 2004. Spatially balanced sampling of natural resources. Journal of the American Statistical Association 99:262–278.

Tomback D. F. 1982. Dispersal of whitebark pine seeds by Clark's nutcracker: A mutualism hypothesis. Journal of Animal Ecology 51:451–467.

Tomback, D. F., and K. C. Kendall. 2001. Biodiversity losses: the downward spiral. Pages 243–262 *in* D. F. Tomback, S. F. Arno, and R. E. Keane, editors. Whitebark pine communities: Ecology and restoration. Island Press, Washington, D.C.

Tomback, D. F., S. F. Arno, and R. E. Keane. 2001. The compelling case for management intervention. Pages 3–25 *in* D. F. Tomback, S. F. Arno, and R. E. Keane, editors. Whitebark pine communities: Ecology and restoration. Island Press, Washington, D.C.

Tomback, D. F., A. W. Schoettle, K. E. Chevalier, and C. A. Jones. 2005. Life on the Edge for limber pine: Seed dispersal within peripheral population. Ecoscience 12:519-529.

Tomback, D. F., and P. Achuff. 2010. Blister rust and western forest biodiversity: ecology, values, and outlook for white pines. Forest Pathology 40:186-225.

van Mantgem, P. J., N. L. Stephenson, J. C. Byrne, L. D. Daniels, J. F. Franklin, P. Z. Fulé, M. E. Harmon, A. J. Larson, J. M. Smith, A. H. Taylor, and others. 2009. Widespread increase of tree mortality rates in the western United States. Science 323:521–523.

Woodhouse, C. A., G. T. Pederson, and S. T. Gray. 2011. An 1800-yr record of decadal-scale hydroclimatic variability in the upper Arkansas River basin from bristlecone pine. Quaternary Research 75: 483-490.

Appendix 1

Table A-1. List of sampling locations for white pine monitoring plots in the SIEN. The column EvalStatus indicates whether a site was established, dropped because it was non-target, or if it was not established (not visited) in the field. Oversample locations provide the replacements for sites dropped during office and field evaluation. Oversample sites 49 and 51-54 will become permanent members of panel 1. Note that UTM X and UTM Y are the plot corner 1 coordinates as established in the field, and no longer match exactly the coordinates produced by the GRTS algorithm used to navigate to the plot during initial set-up.

Park-Species	Plot ID	UTM X	UTM Y	panel	EvalStatus	EvalNotes
YOSE-PIAL	01	272730	4211038	Panel_1	Dropped	No trees
YOSE-PIAL	02	288803	4213209	Panel_1	Not Established	
YOSE-PIAL	03	296086	4182246	Panel_1	Established	
YOSE-PIAL	04	290565	4185337	Panel_1	Established	
YOSE-PIAL	05	285267	4218542	Panel_1	Dropped	No trees
YOSE-PIAL	06	279028	4195054	Panel_1	Not Established	
YOSE-PIAL	07	286346	4191034	Panel_1	Established	
YOSE-PIAL	08	295118	4177652	Panel_1	Established	
YOSE-PIAL	09	289361	4208460	Panel_1	Dropped	No trees
YOSE-PIAL	10	296147	4197449	Panel_1	Established	
YOSE-PIAL	11	265845	4218338	Panel_1	Not Established	
YOSE-PIAL	12	265845	4218338	Panel_1	Dropped	No trees
YOSE-PIAL	13	290527	4215554	Panel_1	Dropped	No trees
YOSE-PIAL	14	298864	4191731	Panel_1	Established	
YOSE-PIAL	15	294711	4185916	Panel_1	Established	
YOSE-PIAL	16	268730	4223677	Panel_1	Not Established	
YOSE-PIAL	49	285782	4214698	OverSamp	Established	Replace site 01
YOSE-PIAL	51	302367	4185091	OverSamp	Not Established	Replace site 05
YOSE-PIAL	52	294468	4174507	OverSamp	Established	Replace site 09
YOSE-PIAL	53	280544	4217606	OverSamp	Established	Replace site 12
YOSE-PIAL	54	297245	4199691	OverSamp	Established	Replace site 13

Park-Species	Plot ID	UTM X	UTM Y	panel	EvalStatus	EvalNotes
SEKI-PIAL	01	367290	4027141	Panel_1	Not Established	
SEKI-PIAL	02	345652	4118340	Panel_1	Not Established	
SEKI-PIAL	03	374534	4075809	Panel_1	Not Established	
SEKI-PIAL	04	375908	4084191	Panel_1	Not Established	
SEKI-PIAL	05	372907	4093446	Panel_1	Not Established	
SEKI-PIAL	06	343590	4112006	Panel_1	Dropped	> 35 degree slope
SEKI-PIAL	07	368793	4067831	Panel_1	Dropped	> 35 degree slope
SEKI-PIAL	08	357644	4085977	Panel_1	Not Established	
SEKI-PIAL	09	366236	4101569	Panel_1	Dropped	> 35 degree slope
SEKI-PIAL	10	364469	4059015	Panel_1	Not Established	
SEKI-PIAL	11	372567	4075392	Panel_1	Not Established	
SEKI-PIAL	12	357551	4083757	Panel_1	Not Established	
SEKI-PIAL	13	360382	4105787	Panel_1	Dropped	No trees
SEKI-PIAL	14	376492	4057576	Panel_1	Rejected in field	No trees
SEKI-PIAL	15	368275	4091574	Panel_1	Not Established	
SEKI-PIAL	16	356989	4077572	Panel_1	Dropped	> 35 degree slope
SEKI-PIAL	49	367099	4094695	OverSamp	Not Established	Replace site 06
SEKI-PIAL	50	342764	4117298	OverSamp	Dropped	> 35 degree slope
SEKI-PIAL	51	376192	4070336	OverSamp	Not Established	Replace site 07
SEKI-PIAL	52	364852	4084028	OverSamp	Not Established	Replace site 09
SEKI-PIAL	53	363263	4099360	OverSamp	Dropped	No trees
SEKI-PIAL	54	338892	4118855	OverSamp	Not Established	Replace site 13
SEKI-PIAL	55	368946	4075659	OverSamp	Dropped	> 35 degree slope
SEKI-PIAL	56	359700	4080686	OverSamp	Dropped	> 35 degree slope
SEKI-PIAL	57	359051	4104460	OverSamp	Not Established	Replace site 16

Park-Species	Plot ID	UTM X	UTM Y	panel	EvalStatus	EvalNotes
SEKI-PIBA	01	355125	4029380	Panel_1	Not Established	
SEKI-PIBA	02	375719	4039071	Panel_1	Established	
SEKI-PIBA	03	363290	4043329	Panel_1	Not Established	
SEKI-PIBA	04	362613	4067179	Panel_1	Not Established	
SEKI-PIBA	05	370614	4026162	Panel_1	No Established	
SEKI-PIBA	06	376987	4042808	Panel_1	Established	
SEKI-PIBA	07	374790	4056572	Panel_1	Established	
SEKI-PIBA	08	362507	4062625	Panel_1	Not Established	
SEKI-PIBA	09	377825	4033524	Panel_1	Established	
SEKI-PIBA	10	380915	4038348	Panel_1	Established	
SEKI-PIBA	11	375678	4050112	Panel_1	Established	
SEKI-PIBA	12	367915	4076906	Panel_1	Not Established	
SEKI-PIBA	13	363692	4033498	Panel_1	Not Established	
SEKI-PIBA	14	366283	4038676	Panel_1	Dropped	> 35 degree slope
SEKI-PIBA	15	386319	4040888	Panel_1	Established	
SEKI-PIBA	16	356738	4061064	Panel_1	Not Established	
SEKI-PIBA	49	370595	4020664	OverSamp	Not Established	Replace site 14

www.ingramcontent.com/pod-product-compliance
Lightning Source LLC
Chambersburg PA
CBHW080940290526
45795CB00007BA/2832